Guided by Grace

"A Mother's Legacy of Love and Divine Breakthrough"

By

Apostle Asia Roberts

Guided by Grace

"A Mother's Legacy of Love and Divine Breakthrough"

© Copyright 2025 by Apostle Asia Roberts.
All Rights Reserved

Published by Corner Stone International Enterprises

978-1-967875-00-9

DEDICATION

This book is dedicated to:

All the mothers, who walk through the seasons of life with grace as their guide, faith as their compass, and love as their legacy.

May you find strength in His divine promises, courage in the breakthroughs yet to come, and peace in knowing that your labor of love leaves footprints of eternity.

This book is lovingly dedicated to the tireless hands, the praying hearts, and the enduring spirits of mothers everywhere.

You are the reflection of God's infinite grace.

Special Dedication

To my beloved mother, Evangelist Marie Roberts,

Your love, sacrifice, and unwavering dedication have shaped the lives of your five children and laid the foundation for their faith and purpose. With every prayer you lifted, every lesson you imparted, and every act of love you gave, you poured yourself into the lives entrusted to your care, leaving a legacy that reflects the very heart of God.

You taught us to walk in faith, to embrace grace, and to trust in the One who holds all things together. Your devotion to raising us in the light of His Word has not only impacted our lives but also touched the lives of countless others. Your strength in times of trial, your compassion in moments of need, and your endless love have been a guiding light and an inspiration to us all.

This dedication is a tribute to you, a mother whose love mirrors the eternal love of our Heavenly Father. Thank you for walking boldly in your calling, for sowing seeds of grace and faith, and for leaving behind a legacy that will forever glorify the Kingdom of God.

With all my love and gratitude,

Asia Roberts

Table of Contents

DEDICATION 3

Special Dedication 4

Table of Contents 6

Forward: A Message from the Holy Spirit . 7

Preface 9

Introduction 11

Chapter One: Spring - The Seeds of Grace 14

Chapter Two: Summer – Walking by the Divine Compass 18

Chapter Three: Autumn – A Legacy of Love 22

Chapter Four: Winter – Grace Through Trials 26

Conclusion 30

Call to Action 32

Invitation to Accept Jesus as Lord and Savior 35

A Special Message to My Daughters and Spiritual Daughters 39

About the Author 41

Forward: A Message from the Holy Spirit

Beloved,

I am with you, guiding, nurturing, and sustaining you through every season of your life. Just as the wind carries the whispers of grace, so too does My presence go before you, clearing the way for divine opportunities and breakthroughs.

To you, dear mothers, I have given a sacred calling. Your love mirrors My own, infinite and enduring. Your faith anchors your family, and your prayers ascend like incense, drawing Heaven's attention. You are vessels of My grace, and through you, I pour out blessings upon generations.

In moments of strength and in moments of weariness, remember this: My grace is sufficient for you. Trust in My voice to guide you, for I am your compass in every storm and your light in every valley. Lean into Me, and I will show you the path to walk.

You are never alone. My love surrounds you, My wisdom directs you, and My power strengthens you. The seeds you sow in love and faith will yield a harvest that glorifies the Kingdom. This is your legacy, a legacy born of My Spirit working through you.

Go forth in joy and confidence, knowing that you are chosen, cherished, and equipped for all that I have called you to do.

With Agape and grace,

The Holy Spirit

Preface

The journey of motherhood is sacred, filled with moments of joy, sacrifice, faith, and unending love. It is a calling that weaves together divine purpose and human experience, showcasing the grace of God in every season. This book, "Guided by Grace: A Mother's Legacy of Love and Divine Breakthrough," was written to honor that calling and to celebrate the unique ways God uses mothers to shape the world through their faith and love.

As you read, you will discover stories of grace during life's challenges, the power of trusting in God's divine compass, and the enduring legacy of love that mothers leave for future generations. Each chapter is an invitation to reflect on your journey, to embrace the grace that sustains you, and to recognize the breakthroughs that await you through the Holy Spirit's guidance.

This book is not just for mothers but for anyone who has been touched by a mother's love or inspired by her faith. It is a testament to the truth that God's grace is sufficient in every season and that He uses the ordinary to accomplish the extraordinary.

May this book remind you that you are chosen, cherished, and empowered by God. As you turn these pages, may you find encouragement, inspiration, and a deeper connection with the One who lovingly walks beside you through every season of life.

With Agape and Blessings,

Apostle Asia Roberts

Introduction

Motherhood is more than a role it is a divine calling, a sacred journey through which God's grace is revealed in the most profound and intimate ways. It is in the moments of laughter, the silent prayers in the midnight hour, and the resilience in the face of challenges that motherhood becomes a reflection of God's unconditional love and unyielding strength.

This book, Guided by Grace: A Mother's Legacy of Love and Divine Breakthrough, is a celebration of the incredible journey that mothers undertake, a journey that is not just physical or emotional, but deeply spiritual. It is a journey marked by seasons each with its own beauty, lessons, and opportunities to witness the miraculous power of God at work.

In the spring, mothers plant seeds of faith, hope, and love, trusting that God will bring growth and fruitfulness in due time. In the summer, they walk boldly, guided by the Holy Spirit, as their families flourish under their care.

In the autumn, they reflect on the abundant harvest of their labor, cherishing the legacy they have built through love and sacrifice. And in the winter, they hold steadfastly to God's promises, finding grace even in moments of stillness and waiting.

Through each of these seasons, the Holy Spirit acts as a divine compass, leading and empowering mothers to fulfill their calling with wisdom and strength. God's grace sustains them through trials, His love energizes them in moments of exhaustion, and His divine opportunities remind them that there is always more to come.

This book is not merely a guide; it is a tribute to the extraordinary role that mothers play in the unfolding of God's plan. It is a reminder that, as a mother, you are never alone. The same God who spoke the world into existence walks with you through every step of your journey, equipping you with everything you need to nurture, lead, and inspire.

Whether you are a mother seeking encouragement, someone longing to understand the depth of a mother's love, or a believer eager to explore God's grace in action, this book is for you. Let the words within these pages fill your heart with hope and inspire you to embrace the divine calling of motherhood with renewed faith and joy.

Welcome to a journey of grace, guidance, and legacy. It is my prayer that this book will empower you to see your life through God's eyes full of purpose, beauty, and limitless possibilities.

May this book be a source of inspiration and a testament to the undeniable truth that with God, all things are possible. Let us step forward together, guided by His infinite grace.

Chapter One: Spring - The Seeds of Grace

Spring is a season of new beginnings, a time when the world awakens with life and hope. Just as the earth becomes fertile and ready to bear fruit, so too does the spirit of a mother in this season. It is in the springtime of life that God calls mothers to sow seeds of grace, trusting that He will bring growth and renewal in His perfect timing.

The seeds of grace begin with faith. Faith is the foundation upon which the journey of motherhood is built. In these early stages, mothers must trust that God's grace is sufficient to sustain them through the joys and trials ahead. Grace is not earned; it is freely given by God, and it empowers mothers to face the unknown with confidence and peace.

God's Word reminds us, "For it is by grace you have been saved, through faith, and this is not from yourselves, it is the gift of God" (Ephesians 2:8). Just as a farmer sows seeds with faith in the harvest, so too must mothers sow seeds of prayer, love, and faith, knowing that God will nurture them into something beautiful.

The spring season is also a time for preparation and cultivation. Just as the soil must be tilled and watered to bring forth fruit, so must the heart and mind be prepared to receive God's grace. Mothers are called to remain steadfast in prayer, seeking God's guidance and wisdom in the decisions they make. It is through these acts of faithfulness that God equips mothers to become the spiritual gardeners of their families, tending to the growth and well-being of those entrusted to their care.

In this season, mothers learn the importance of patience. Growth does not happen overnight, and breakthroughs often come in God's perfect timing rather than our own. Just as seeds take time to sprout and mature, the prayers of a mother may take time to bear fruit. Yet, with patience and trust, mothers can find peace in knowing that God is always at work behind the scenes, nurturing and cultivating the seeds of grace.

Spring is also a season of hope. It is a time to dream of the harvest to come, to envision the future filled with divine opportunities and blessings. This hope sustains mothers through challenges and gives them the courage to continue sowing seeds of grace, even when the soil seems dry or the conditions unfavorable.

As you reflect on the spring season of your own life, consider the seeds of grace that God has called you to sow. Are you planting seeds of faith and love in your family? Are you cultivating the soil of your heart through prayer and devotion? Are you trusting God to bring forth growth in His perfect timing?

Remember, every seed sown in grace has the potential to yield a harvest that glorifies the Kingdom of God. Let this season of spring be a time to embrace new beginnings, to sow seeds of grace with faith and hope, and to trust in God's promise of renewal and abundance.

Scripture to reflect upon:

- "Sow righteousness for yourselves, reap the fruit of unfailing love, and break up your unplowed ground; for it is time to seek the Lord, until He comes and showers His righteousness on you." (Hosea 10:12)

- "Let us not become weary in doing good, for at the proper time we will reap a harvest if we do not give up." (Galatians 6:9)

Chapter Two: Summer – Walking by the Divine Compass

Summer is a season of energy, growth, and fulfillment, symbolizing the vibrant, active phase of life where faith matures, and God's guidance becomes even more essential. In this season, mothers are called to embrace the divine compass that God provides, navigating through the opportunities, challenges, and daily rhythms with His wisdom and grace.

The divine compass is the Holy Spirit, who guides us through every decision, every crossroad, and every uncertainty. Just as travelers rely on a physical compass to find their way, so too must mothers rely on the spiritual compass provided by God. It is through surrender and trust in His direction that mothers can confidently lead their families through the busyness of life.

Isaiah 30:21 assures us of this divine guidance: "Whether you turn to the right or to the left, your ears will hear a voice behind you, saying, "This is the way; walk in it." This promise is a source of comfort and assurance for mothers who often find themselves balancing countless responsibilities. God's guidance is perfect, and when we seek Him in prayer, He faithfully reveals the path we are meant to take.

Summer is also a season of movement and momentum. It is a time when families are flourishing, relationships are deepening, and activities abound. In the midst of this active season, the divine compass reminds mothers to pause and seek God's presence. It is easy to become overwhelmed by the demands of life, but God calls mothers to find rest in Him, allowing His Spirit to refresh and renew them for the journey ahead.

Proverbs 3:5-6 offers timeless wisdom for this season: "Trust in the Lord with all your heart and lean not on your own understanding; in all your ways submit to Him, and He will make your paths straight." Trusting God's divine compass requires surrendering our own plans and relying on His perfect wisdom. This act of faith not only brings clarity but also empowers mothers to walk boldly in their calling, knowing they are never alone.

Another aspect of summer is the cultivation of relationships. This season provides opportunities for mothers to nurture bonds with their children, spouses, and communities. The divine compass reminds mothers to lead with love, patience, and understanding, reflecting the fruits of the Spirit in their interactions. Galatians 5:22-23 describes these fruits as "love, joy, peace, forbearance, kindness, goodness, faithfulness, gentleness, and self-control." Walking by the divine compass means allowing these qualities to guide every conversation and every action.

Summer is a season of abundance, but it is also a season of stewardship. Mothers are entrusted with the care and nurturing of their families, and walking by the divine compass ensures that every decision is made with wisdom and purpose. From teaching children about faith to managing the household with grace, mothers can rely on God's guidance to steward their blessings well.

As you reflect on the summer season of your life, consider how the divine compass has guided you. Are you seeking God's direction in your decisions and daily routines? Are you finding moments of rest and renewal in His presence? Are you cultivating relationships with love and grace, allowing the fruits of the Spirit to shine through you?

Remember, walking by the divine compass is not about perfection, it is about faithfulness. God does not expect mothers to have all the answers; He simply calls them to trust in Him and follow His lead. Embrace this season of summer as a time to walk boldly, love deeply, and trust completely in the One who guides you through every step of the journey.

Scripture to reflect upon:

- "I will instruct you and teach you in the way you should go; I will counsel you with my loving eye on you." (Psalm 32:8)

- "The steps of a good man are ordered by the Lord: and he delighteth in his way." (Psalm 37:23)

Chapter Three: Autumn – A Legacy of Love

Autumn is a season of reflection, harvest, and thanksgiving. It is a time when the labor of the past seasons comes to fruition, and the beauty of what has been sown is fully revealed. For mothers, autumn represents the stage in life when the seeds of grace and the trust in God's divine compass yield a legacy of love, a lasting impact that shapes future generations.

The legacy of love begins with the realization that every act of faithfulness, sacrifice, and prayer has meaning. In this season, mothers look back on the ways they have poured themselves into their families, communities, and the world around them. Though the road may not have always been easy, God's grace has been the constant thread, weaving together a beautiful tapestry of love and purpose.

Proverbs 31:28 beautifully capture the essence of this season: "Her children arise and call her blessed; her husband also, and he praises her." The legacy of a mother's love is evident in the lives she has touched, the values she has instilled, and the faith she has inspired. Her influence extends far beyond what she can see, echoing into the future as a testimony to God's faithfulness.

Autumn is also a time to celebrate the harvest. Mothers can take joy in the growth and accomplishments of their children, the strengthening of relationships, and the fulfillment of dreams. This season is not just about looking back but also about appreciating the present blessings that come from years of faith and perseverance.

A legacy of love is not defined by perfection but by consistency and faithfulness. It is about showing up, day after day, with a heart full of grace and a willingness to trust God through every challenge. It is about the moments of quiet prayer, the words of encouragement, and the sacrifices made in love. These are the seeds that bear fruit in the lives of those who are touched by a mother's presence.

The story of Hannah in 1 Samuel 1-2 is a powerful example of a mother's legacy of love. Hannah's faith and devotion to God led her to dedicate her son, Samuel, to the Lord's service. Her legacy was not only reflected in the life of her son but also in the impact Samuel had as a prophet and leader of Israel. Hannah's story reminds us that the love and faithfulness of a mother can have far-reaching and eternal consequences.

Autumn is also a season of gratitude. Mothers are called to give thanks for the journey, recognizing that every trial and triumph has been part of God's divine plan. Gratitude shifts the focus from what has been lost to what has been gained, allowing mothers to see the abundant blessings that have come from their labors of love.

As you reflect on the autumn season of your life, consider the legacy of love you are building. Are you celebrating the harvest of your efforts? Are you giving thanks for the blessings that surround you? Are you continuing to sow seeds of faith and love, knowing that God is not finished with His work in your life?

Remember, the legacy of a mother's love is eternal. It is a reflection of God's love, a beacon of hope for future generations, and a testimony to the power of grace. Embrace this season of autumn as a time to honor the journey, celebrate the harvest, and trust that the seeds you have planted will continue to bear fruit in God's perfect timing.

Scripture to reflect upon:

- "Her children arise and call her blessed; her husband also, and he praises her." (Proverbs 31:28)

- "The righteous will flourish like a palm tree, they will grow like a cedar of Lebanon; planted in the house of the Lord, they will flourish in the courts of our God. They will still bear fruit in old age; they will stay fresh and green." (Psalm 92:12-14)

Chapter Four: Winter – Grace Through Trials

Winter is often seen as a season of stillness, endurance, and quiet preparation. For mothers, the winter of life may represent times of difficulty, waiting, or uncertainty. Yet, it is in this season that God's grace shines most profoundly, sustaining and empowering mothers to persevere through trials and embrace the divine opportunities hidden within them.

Trials, while challenging, are not without purpose. Scripture reminds us that trials refine and strengthen our faith. James 1:2-4 says, "Consider it pure joy, my brothers and sisters, whenever you face trials of many kinds, because you know that the testing of your faith produces perseverance. Let perseverance finish its work so that you may be mature and complete, not lacking anything. Winter is a season where perseverance is cultivated, and God's grace is revealed as a source of strength, comfort, and growth.

In this season, mothers may encounter moments of stillness, times when prayers seem unanswered, and progress feels halted. Yet, winter is not a time of abandonment; it is a time of preparation. Just as seeds lie dormant beneath the snow, awaiting the warmth of spring, so too does God work behind the scenes to bring forth new life and opportunities. His grace sustains us during these quiet times, reminding us that He is always faithful, and His timing is perfect.

Paul's words in 2 Corinthians 12:9 offer hope during the trials of winter: "My grace is sufficient for you, for my power is made perfect in weakness." These words invite mothers to lean into God's grace during moments of weariness, trusting that His strength will carry them through. The power of grace is not dependent on circumstances; it transcends them, offering peace and hope in the midst of uncertainty.

Winter is also a season of spiritual depth. It is a time to draw closer to God, seeking His presence and listening for His voice. Mothers can find solace in prayer and worship, allowing God to refresh their spirits and renew their faith.

Psalm 46:10 encourages us: "Be still and know that I am God." This stillness is not inactivity; it is an intentional posture of trust and surrender, knowing that God is in control.

Grace through trials also manifests in the ability to find joy and gratitude, even in the coldest seasons of life. God's promises remain steadfast, and His love is unchanging. As mothers embrace the winter season, they can find beauty in the quiet moments, reflecting on His faithfulness and trusting in His plan. Romans 8:28 reassures us: "And we know that in all things God works for the good of those who love Him, who have been called according to His purpose."

As you reflect on the winter season of your life, consider how God's grace has sustained you through trials. Have you found moments of stillness to draw closer to Him? Have you allowed His strength to carry you during times of weakness? Have you trusted in His promises, knowing that spring will surely come?

Remember, winter is not the end, it is a season of renewal and preparation for the breakthroughs that lie ahead. God's grace is your constant companion, and His love is your unshakable foundation. Embrace this season as a time to rest in His presence, grow in faith, and trust in the divine opportunities awaiting you.

Scripture to reflect upon:

- "My grace is sufficient for you, for my power is made perfect in weakness." (2 Corinthians 12:9)

- "Be still and know that I am God." (Psalm 46:10)

- "And we know that in all things God works for the good of those who love Him, who have been called according to His purpose." (Romans 8:28)

Conclusion

Life is a journey woven with seasons, each one bringing its own lessons, challenges, and blessings. For mothers, these seasons are profound and sacred, revealing God's grace in every moment. Through the spring of planting seeds of faith, the summer of walking boldly by the divine compass, the autumn of celebrating a legacy of love, and the winter of finding grace through trials, motherhood becomes a testament to the power of God's unfailing love and faithfulness.

This journey is not without its struggles, but it is through these very struggles that God's grace is most profoundly revealed. His grace sustains in moments of weakness, His guidance leads in times of uncertainty, and His love transforms even the smallest acts of faithfulness into an eternal legacy. Every prayer, every sacrifice, and every step of faith is seen and cherished by the One who called you to this sacred role.

As you close this book, may you be reminded that you are never alone on this journey. The Holy Spirit walks beside you as your guide and comforter. His voice whispers encouragement in the quiet moments, and His strength empowers you to persevere through every challenge. Trust in His promises, lean into His grace, and know that your labor of love is not in vain.

You are a reflection of God's heart, a vessel of His grace, and a builder of His Kingdom. Through your faith, love, and trust in Him, you are leaving a legacy that will echo for generations to come. Embrace each season of your life with courage and gratitude, knowing that you are equipped by the Creator to fulfill the divine calling placed on your life.

May this journey of grace inspire you to walk boldly, love deeply, and trust completely in the One who holds all seasons in His hands. Let your life be a testimony to the power of God's grace and a beacon of hope for those who come after you.

Call to Action

Beloved mothers and readers, your journey is one of purpose, beauty, and divine calling. As you reflect on the seasons of grace, let this be your moment to step boldly into the path God has designed for you. Trust in His guidance, embrace His grace, and sow seeds of faith and love that will impact generations to come.

Take this opportunity to deepen your connection with God, to rely on His divine compass, and to leave behind a legacy of love that reflects His eternal glory. Whatever season you find yourself in, know that God's promises are steadfast, His grace is sufficient, and His love is unchanging. Let your life be a testament to His power, a beacon of hope, and an example of faithfulness.

You are chosen. You are cherished. You are equipped. Walk boldly in your calling, and trust that God's grace will lead you to breakthroughs and blessings beyond what you can imagine.

Affirmations:

1. I am guided by the Holy Spirit, and His grace is sufficient for me.

2. I walk in faith and trust, knowing that God's compass leads me on the right path.

3. I sow seeds of love, faith, and righteousness, trusting in God's promise of an abundant harvest.

4. I am strong and capable, empowered by God's grace to fulfill my divine purpose.

5. I embrace every season of life with gratitude, knowing that God is with me through trials and triumphs.

6. My legacy of love reflects God's heart and touches the lives of those around me.

7. I trust in God's timing and plan, knowing that His divine opportunities are always unfolding.

8. I am a vessel of God's grace, called to impact my family and community with love and faith.

9. I find joy in every moment, knowing that God's promises are true and everlasting.

10. I am never alone; the Holy Spirit walks beside me, guiding and strengthening me.

Invitation to Accept Jesus as Lord and Savior

Dear Mothers,

In the midst of your sacred journey, filled with the joys and challenges of motherhood, there is an invitation extended to you that holds eternal significance, an invitation to accept Jesus Christ as your Lord and Savior.

Motherhood is a divine calling, but it is not without its burdens. There are moments of uncertainty, weariness, and longing for guidance that surpass human understanding. As a mother, you pour your heart into your children, your family, and your community, often giving without pause. But even the strongest mother needs the strength and peace that only Jesus can provide.

Jesus calls to you with open arms, saying, "Come to me, all you who are weary and burdened, and I will give you rest" (Matthew 11:28). His love is unconditional, His grace is limitless, and His guidance is perfect. When you accept Him into your heart, you are no longer walking alone. His Spirit becomes your constant companion, equipping you with the wisdom, patience, and strength you need to fulfill your calling as a mother.

Through a relationship with Jesus, you are empowered to reflect His love to your children and leave a legacy of faith that will echo for generations. You are reminded of your worth as a cherished daughter of the King and given the assurance that, no matter what trials come, His grace is sufficient for you.

If you feel the Holy Spirit stirring in your heart today, I encourage you to take this step of faith. Pray this prayer from the depths of your heart:

Prayer of Salvation

"Lord Jesus, I come before You, acknowledging my need for Your love and forgiveness. I believe that You died on the cross for my sins and rose again, offering me eternal life. I accept You as my Lord and Savior, and I surrender my life to You. Fill my heart with Your Spirit, guide me in my journey as a mother, and help me to reflect Your grace and love in all that I do. Thank You for saving me and for giving me new life in You. Amen."

A Mother's Need for Jesus

Motherhood is a reflection of God's heart, a role filled with love, sacrifice, and immeasurable joy. But as a mother, you also bear the weight of nurturing, guiding, and protecting your children. To do this well, you need the strength, wisdom, and peace that come from being rooted in Christ.

Jesus is the source of everything a mother needs. When you are tired, He gives you rest. When you are overwhelmed, He offers peace. When you feel uncertain, His Word provides wisdom and direction. And when you wonder if your efforts are enough, He reminds you that His grace is sufficient, and His strength is made perfect in weakness.

By walking with Jesus, you are not only transformed as an individual but also empowered to lead your children into a life of faith and purpose. You become a living example of His love, teaching your children to rely on Him in all things. Accepting Jesus is not just a personal decision; it is the foundation for building a legacy of faith for your family.

If you have not yet accepted Jesus as your Savior, now is the perfect time. He is waiting to walk with you, guide you, and fill your life with His unending love and grace. He longs to partner with you in this sacred journey of motherhood, equipping you to nurture your children not only in body and mind but also in spirit.

Embrace this moment of grace, and watch as God transforms your heart, your family, and your legacy. He is calling you, are you ready to answer?

A Special Message to My Daughters and Spiritual Daughters

Beloved daughters,

You carry within you a beauty and strength that reflects the very heart of God. Whether you have stepped into the sacred role of motherhood or are awaiting the divine timing for this assignment, know that you are chosen, cherished, and equipped by the Creator to fulfill His extraordinary purpose for your life.

To those who are mothers: Embrace this calling with grace and confidence. The love you pour into your children, the prayers you lift up, and the sacrifices you make are eternal seeds sown into the soil of their lives. You are not alone in this journey. The Holy Spirit is your guide, your comfort, and your strength, empowering you to lead with wisdom and nurture with love. Your impact goes beyond what you can see, and your legacy of faith and love will echo through generations.

To those who desire this assignment: Your longing is seen by the One who created you. Trust in His timing and His plans, for He knows the desires of your heart and delights in fulfilling them. Prepare yourself in faith, knowing that God equips those He calls. Whether biological or spiritual motherhood is His purpose for you, the love and grace you have to offer will bless and transform the lives you touch.

You are daughters of the King, called to walk boldly and love deeply. No matter where you are in your journey, hold fast to His promises. His grace is sufficient for you, His guidance is perfect, and His love is unchanging. Rest in Him, draw strength from His presence, and trust that He Is working all things together for your good.

Remember, you are not defined by the challenges you face but by the faith you carry and the love you give. You are His masterpiece, a reflection of His glory, and a beacon of hope to those around you. Walk forward in confidence, knowing that He has called you to this moment and prepared you for every season to come. With Agape and blessings, Apostle Asia Roberts-Francis

About the Author

Apostle Asia Roberts-Francis is a devoted servant of God, a compassionate leader, and a tireless advocate for spiritual growth and transformation. Her life is a testament to the power of faith, grace, and love, and her ministry has touched countless lives across generations.

As a mother and grandmother, Apostle Roberts understands the sacred role of nurturing and guiding her family with faith and strength. She exemplifies what it means to sow seeds of love and grace, leaving a lasting legacy for her children and grandchildren. Her role as a spiritual mother extends far beyond her own family, as she has become a source of wisdom and encouragement for many in her community and beyond.

With a heart for mentoring and teaching, Apostle Roberts has dedicated her life to walking alongside others in their spiritual journeys. She carries the mantle of leadership with humility, empowering those under her care to embrace their God-given purpose and step boldly into their calling. Her ministry is marked by a deep commitment to sharing the truths of God's Word and equipping believers to experience divine breakthroughs and opportunities.

Through her writings, Apostle Roberts brings forth messages of hope, encouragement, and empowerment, anchored in the Scriptures and inspired by the Holy Spirit. She has a gift for connecting deeply with her readers, weaving spiritual truths into relatable and transformative teachings.

Apostle Asia Roberts is a voice of grace in every season, a pillar of faith in times of uncertainty, and a beacon of love for those seeking to grow in their relationship with God. Her legacy as a mother, grandmother, and spiritual mother continues to inspire and bless the lives of many, making her an invaluable guide to navigating the seasons of grace.

Authorship: Apostle Asia has authored several impactful books, including

1. "Changing the Atmosphere: Living at a Kingdom Standard"
2. "Embrace: A Journey Within"
3. "Embracing God's Acceptance: Breaking Free From Rejection"
4. "Embracing Singleness and Fulfillment: A Journey of Purpose"
5. "Jesus Portrayed In The Gospels"
6. "An Account of the Life of the Apostle Paul"
7. Victory Over Lust: A Biblical Guide To Purity
8. Perseverance Unveiled: The Blessings and Benefits of Endurance

9. The Transformative Power of Love: A Journey Through Scripture and Life

10. Relax, Relate, Release: A Biblical Journey to Peace

11. Angels in God's Divine Work

12. A Love Story Like No Other

13. The Anointed Queen: Embracing The Spirit and Legacy of Queen Sheba

14. The Holy Spirit as Our Compass: Navigating the Year of Breakthrough and Divine Opportunities

15. Cultivating Internal Character

16. Do Not Chase After Blessings: A Journey of Covenant With God

17. Seated in Heavenly Places

18. The Season of Restoration and Divine Promotion

19. Fortitude Standing Strong In Adversity

20. Divine Destiny: A Journey of Purpose and Potential

21. The Power of Prayer Watches: Unlocking Divine Timing and Revelation

22. Guarding the Heart:

23. Embracing God's Grace In Our Lives and many more....

Apostle Asia Roberts-Francis not only stands as a vibrant thread in the tapestry of faith but also extends her talents to assist other authors. Here are the services she offers:

1. **Ghostwriting:**

    As a skilled ghostwriter, Apostle Asia can breathe life into your ideas, crafting a complete manuscript that reflects your voice and vision. Whether you have extensive notes or just a vague concept, she can transform it into a compelling book.

2. Publishing Services:

If you are seeking to publish your work, Apostle Asia can guide you through the process. She understands the intricacies of the publishing industry and can help you navigate self-publishing or traditional publishing routes.

3. Editing:

An essential step in any book's journey, editing ensures your manuscript shines. Apostle Asia offers professional editing services, addressing grammar, structure, plot, and character development. Whether you are self-publishing or aiming for a traditional publishing deal, an editor is crucial.

4. Proofreading

The final polish before publication, proofreading catches those pesky typos, inconsistencies, and formatting errors. Apostle Asia's keen eye ensures your book is pristine and ready for readers.

5. **Paraphrasing:**

   Sometimes, existing content needs a fresh perspective. Apostle Asia can rephrase and reword text, making it more engaging and impactful.

6. **Book Cover Art and Design:**

   Ensuring your book has a captivating and professional appearance that attracts readers.

Whether you are an aspiring author or an established one, Apostle Asia Roberts-Francis offers her expertise to elevate your literary journey.

Follow Apostle Asia on Tik Tok, her social media platforms and Amazon Author

Page
https://www.amazon.com/author/apostleasiaroberts

www.ingramcontent.com/pod-product-compliance
Lightning Source LLC
Chambersburg PA
CBHW060035180426
43196CB00045B/2690